Chuck Close
The Magnolia Tapestry Project

CHUCK CLOSE
THE MAGNOLIA TAPESTRY PROJECT

MAGNOLIA EDITIONS

2527 Magnolia St
Oakland, CA 94607
http://www.magnoliaeditions.com

ISBN 978-0-9799164-1-0

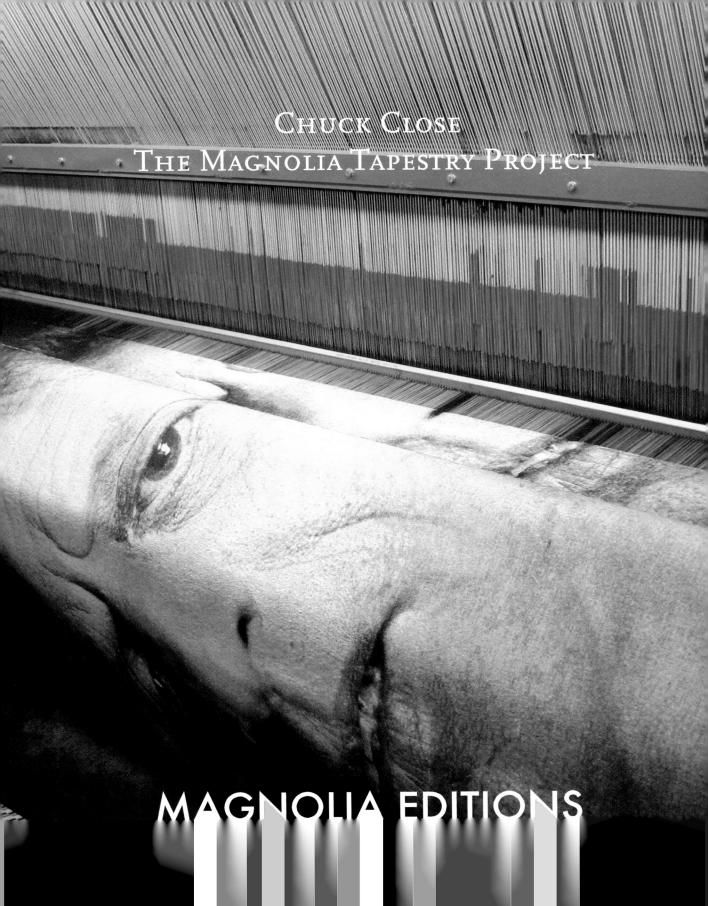

Self Portrait
2007
103 x 79 in.
Edition of 10

The technology of mark-making has experienced a rapid acceleration since the turn of the 19th century, due in large part to discoveries and innovations in the field of weaving: a direct line can be traced from the punch-card system of the Jacquard loom and early breakthroughs in color theory to today's computers and LCD displays. The Magnolia Tapestry Project brings this lineage full circle by applying contemporary computing sophistication and lessons learned in the studio to the Jacquard weaving process. A look at the origin of the project reveals the importance of both the powerful computing technology of today and a constellation of innovators stretching back into history; that Chuck Close, an intrepid explorer of media both antique and cutting-edge, would be a vanguard of tapestry innovation seems highly appropriate in light of this interplay of old and new processes.

Two detail views of Close's color *Self Portrait*.

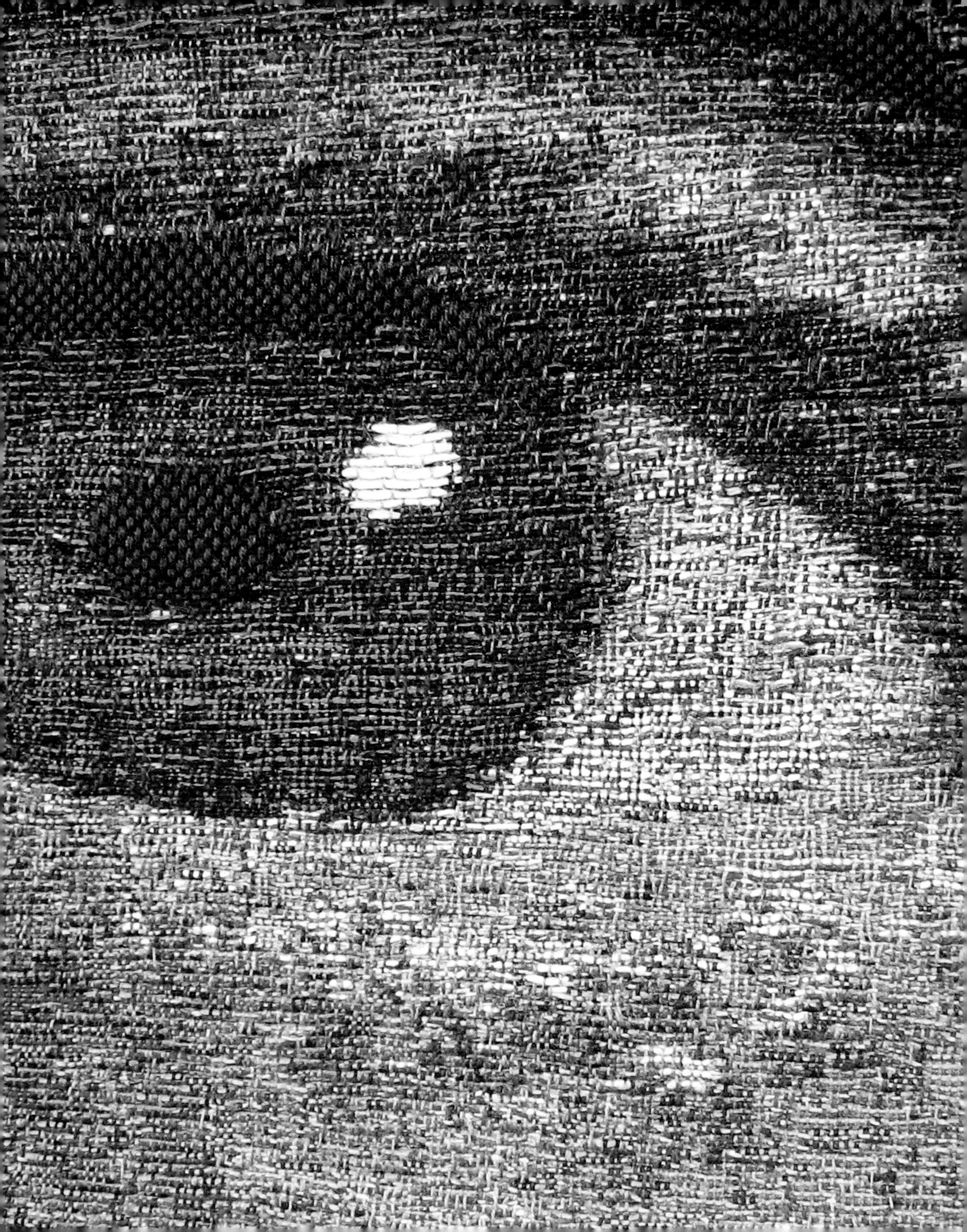

Self Portrait
2006
103 x 79 in.
Edition of 10

The tapestry medium itself is ancient; for more than two thousand years its popularity has waxed and waned, its status shifting between folk art and fine art, imperial status symbol and industrially produced furnishing, depending on the cultural moment. The process of combining warp and weft threads is a creative module nearly as old as the pigments on the walls of the Lascaux caves; the history of tapestry stretches from Penelope and Odysseus to mass-produced automobile interiors. The Jacquard punch card system, first presented (by most accounts) in 1801, revolutionized the medium while at the same time providing the basis for the development of computer technology in the early 20th century. The binary "memory" of Jacquard's perforated cards was the progenitor of other machines with programmed functions: the player piano, the adding machine, and eventually, the computer. The term Luddite, often used to describe contemporary technophobes, refers to the 19th century textile workers who tried to destroy Jacquard's device at its first unveiling.

Philip Glass State II

2006

103 x 79 in.

Edition of 6

In Jacquard weaving, the repeating series of multicolored warp and weft threads of which tapestries are comprised can be used to create colors that are optically blended – i.e., the human eye apprehends the threads' combination of values as a single color. This method can be likened to pointillism, a style of painting in which tiny dots or points placed in close proximity are optically blended as described above. In fact, pointillism originated from discoveries made in the tapestry medium: the style's emergence in the 19th century can be traced to the influence of Eugène Chevreul, a French chemist responsible for developing the color wheel of primary and intermediary hues. Chevreul worked as the director of the dye works at Les Gobelins tapestry works in Paris, where he noticed that the perceived color of a particular thread was influenced by its surrounding threads, a phenomenon he called "simultaneous contrast." Chevreul's work, itself a continuation of theories of color elaborated by Leonardo da Vinci and Goethe, influenced painters including Eugène Delacroix and Georges Seurat. The principles articulated by Chevreul also apply to contemporary television and computer displays, which use tiny dots of red, green and blue to render color. The creation of an apparently seamless image through the use of repeated variations on a single tiny module will also be familiar to anyone who has experienced Close's previous works involving fingerprints, dots, brush strokes, et al.

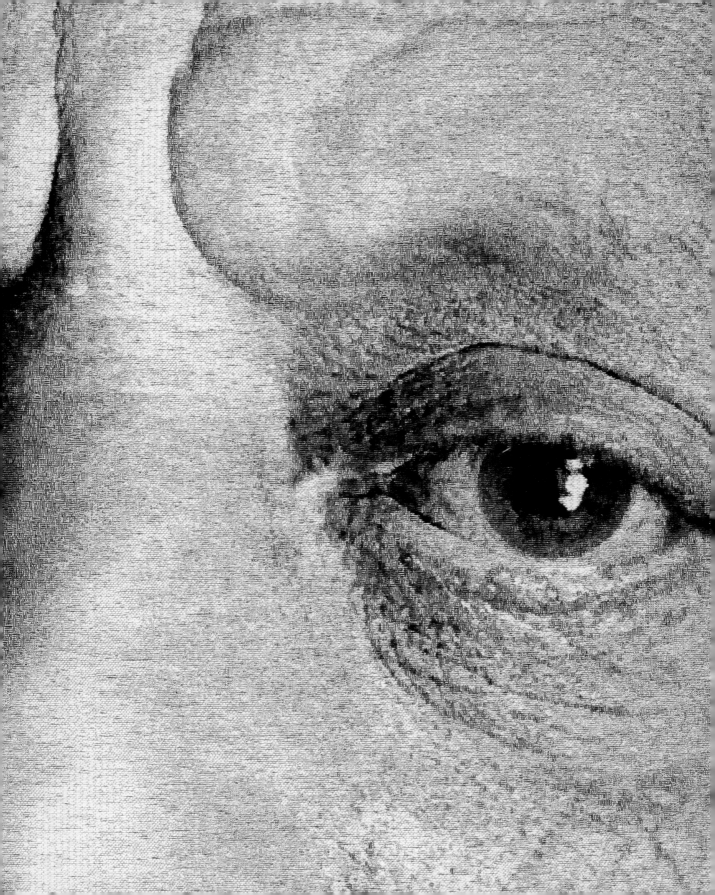

Experimental innovations in portraiture have been Close's trademark for nearly half a century. In 2005, the artist teamed with the Magnolia Tapestry Project to begin a series of limited-edition woven textiles; his first edition depicts his longtime friend, the composer Philip Glass. The parallel aspects of the pair's philosophies and techniques are evident even at a glance: just as Close's portraits are built from slight tonal variations on a single module – whether a fingerprint, a pointillist dot, a brushstroke or warp and weft threads – many of Glass's best-known works feature hypnotic repetitions of spare arpeggios: reiterated, shifting motifs which add up to more than the sum of their parts. Close is often associated with painting and photography, but has conducted rigorous explorations of countless media; likewise, while generally linked to the world of classical and avant-garde composition, Glass has worked in a staggering number of musical idioms, innovating and redefining boundaries in projects ranging from operas to film scores to pop songs.

Philip Glass on the loom.

Philip Glass with Kiki at Aperture Gallery, NYC in 2006.

Philip Glass with tapestries by WIlliam Wiley, April Gornik and Martha Erlebacher at Sullivan Goss, Santa Barbara, CA in 2006.

Philip Glass with tapestries by Katherine Westerhout, Rupert Garcia, Squeak Carnwath and John Nava at the Bedford Gallery, Walnut Creek, CA in 2005.

The majority of Close's tapestries to date are based on a series of daguerreotype portraits created in collaboration with Jerry Spagnoli within the last decade. The gilded, silver-coated daguerreotype plates are scanned at high resolution by Adamson Editions in Washington, D.C.; the scans are then converted by Close and Magnolia Editions director Donald Farnsworth into digital "weave files." In the process of developing custom color palettes for a given image, which – in the case of Close's black and white daguerreotypes – requires the accurate assembly of 500 shades of woven whites, grays, and blacks, a digital sphere spectrometer (an alien technology to most weavers) is used to determine which optically blended colors will emerge when the threads are combined. The Magnolia Tapestry Project method of identifying and assigning woven colors, developed by Farnsworth and artist John Nava, might be likened to a painter mixing 500 unique and precise hues via a lengthy process of measurement, calculation, and experimentation, with a host of additional variables such as differing weave structures and the optical interaction of adjacent color combinations providing complications and challenges at every step. As with any of his other projects, Close has control over each pixel of the weave file, ensuring complete fidelity to what might anachronistically be referred to as 'the artist's hand.' A series of proofs are woven for each edition, and Close supervises revisions to palettes and weave files until every thread of each edition reflects his artistic intent.

Experimental test weavings for Close's color *Self Portrait*.

The weave files are woven at a mill in Belgium on a seven-foot wide, double-headed electronic Jacquard on a customized Dornier loom, utilizing 17,800 warp threads of repeating groups of 8 colors. The mill is operated by the de Keukelara family, whose great-grandfather sold hand-loomed weavings to wholesalers in the famous Bruges bell tower. The family is steeped in a rich tradition of Flemish weaving; yet in keeping with the spirit of the Magnolia Tapestry Project, it was the de Keukelara's willingness to defy that tradition which would ultimately result in the reconfiguration of weaving technology into a powerful tool for artists such as Close. In 1992, brothers Roland and Christian de Keukelara broke with conventional hand and automatic loom techniques when they set up a 90 cm loom and paper punch card Jacquard as an experiment, wholly independent of their commercial weaving business. The brothers believed that they could use this experimental loom to produce a Jacquard tapestry comprised of 8 warp threads and 8 weft thread colors, for a total of 65 shots per cm. Three years and countless tests, adjustments, and refinements later, the de Keukelaras successfully realized their 65 shots per cm weaving technique. Encouraged by this breakthrough, the brothers then moved to Wielsbeke and set up an even more extraordinary weaving machine: a 2 m 20 cm Dornier loom, built to custom strength specifications. The loom's warp threads are controlled by 17,800 corresponding electromagnetic lifters which, guided by the Magnolia Tapestry Project's weave files, rise or fall like the keys on a player piano. These lifters are driven by the most powerful motor possible, housed upstairs in a separate steel superstructure. This "hot rod" loom, in combination with the innovative color techniques developed by the Magnolia Tapestry Project, opened the door for the revitalization of the tapestry medium. To weave Close's black and white daguerreotypes, the Magnolia Tapestry Project and the weavers pushed the process even further: the weft threads in Close's tapestries are comprised of not 8 but 10 repeating colors, chosen by Farnsworth specifically for Close daguerreotypes, woven at 75 shots per cm, for a total of 190 weft threads per inch.

Tests for Close's *Self Portrait* on the loom.

Detail view of surface of color *Self Portrait*.

Lyle
2006
103 x 79 in.
Edition of 6

The genesis of Close's tapestries lies in the convergence of innovative, sometimes iconoclastic thinkers – from Jacquard to Chevreul, the de Keukelara brothers, Farnsworth, and Close himself – with the application of powerful and unorthodox technologies. The tapestries represent something akin to an alchemical transformation: the intimacy of Close's photographs is preserved, even amplified, while the medium itself is wholly metamorphosed, from silver crystals to woven fibers. At the same time, these works extend Close's career-long exploration of the tension between artifice and realism: i.e., using a highly artificial surface to compose an image which resonates in a familiar way with the reality and life experiences of its audience. Despite the myriad difficulties which artists face at this point in history, the mere fact that ones and zeroes can be sent around the world to direct industrial technology in the creation of works of art such as Close's tapestries suggests that this is an exciting time to be an artist. At the first display in Belgium of works created using Farnsworth and Nava's process, a 2001 exhibition of tapestries by Nava at the Bruges bell tower, the president of Dornier mused, "I didn't know our looms were capable of this." Just as Close has developed numerous unprecedented techniques (for example, his use of 30,000 watt lights) to reinvent portraiture, the Magnolia Tapestry Project is using the tools of the digital age to breathe new life into the ancient paradigm of warp and weft. Through the dialogue of historical and cutting-edge mark-making processes, the visions of innovators like Close can be realized with a precision and technological wizardry underpinned by a perpetual conversation between the past and the future.

With the exception of *Sunflower*, Close's black and white portraits depict prominent figures in the art world, most of whom are based in New York. Lyle Ashton Harris is a photographer and performer who creates emotionally stirring portraits; Harris often appears as a cipher in his own work, posing with costumes and props to depict characters with powerful cultural associations.

Andres
2006
103 x 79 in.
Edition of 6

Andres Serrano is a photographer; in his own words, his pictures of corpses, religious iconography, Klansmen and the homeless "monumentalize [and] aestheticize the mundane."

Cindy
2006
103 x 79 in.
Edition of 6

Cindy Sherman is a photographer best known for a career-long series of dramatic self-portraits in which she transforms into various characters and archetypes.

Lorna
2006
103 x 79 in.
Edition of 6

Artist Lorna Simpson's photographs and videos examine questions of ethics, identity, and culturally assigned roles.

Renée
2007
103 x 79 in.

Renée Fleming is an American-born opera and Broadway star who is generally considered to be one of the world's finest lyric sopranos. *Renée* was created exclusively for the New York Metropolitan Opera's 2007 "Art for Opera" auction, proceeds from which will support new productions.

Kiki
2006
103 x 79 in.
Edition of 6

Kiki Smith is a sculptor who often addresses corporeal sensuality and the human body in media including wax, bronze and paper.

Sir Elton
2007
103 x 79 in.
Edition of 1

Sir Elton John is an extraordinarily influential, five-time Grammy-winning English composer and performer.

Kate
2007
103 x 79 in.
Edition of 10

Kate Moss is a fashion icon: known primarily as a supermodel, she is also a musician and a designer.

Sunflower
2007
103 x 79 in.
Edition of 10

Describing Close's process, Philip Glass notes: *With this kind of direction, you don't really run out of things to do. That would be like saying the world runs out of ways of being interesting. The material world is always interesting.*

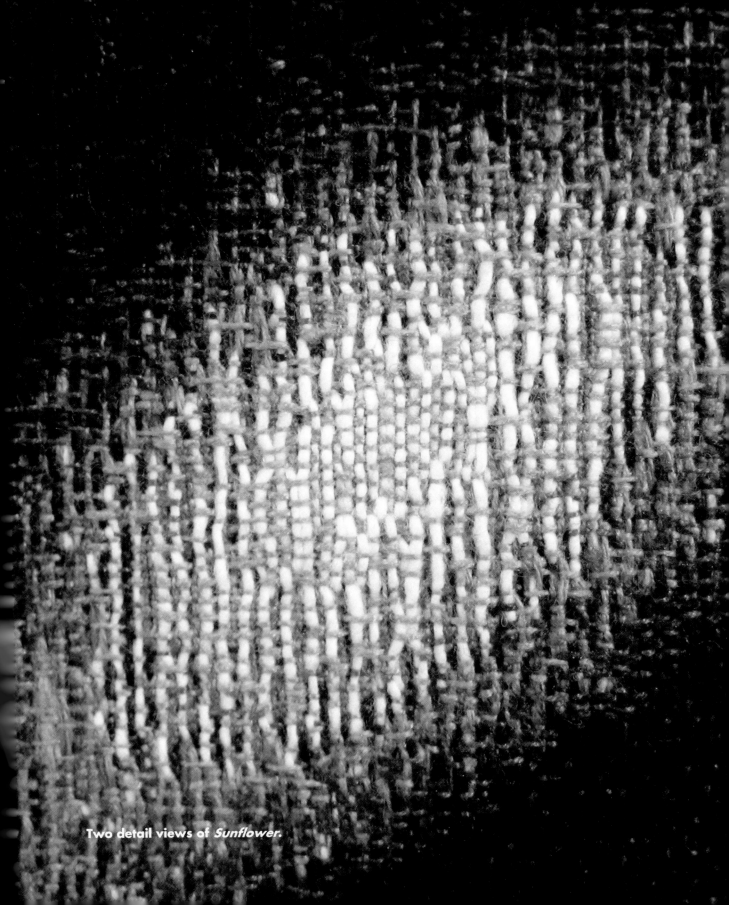

Two detail views of *Sunflower*.